never put down your pen
(a masterpiece of brokenness)

April 2019
Published by:

Printed in the United States of America
Editor: Sunni Soper
Cover: Christopher Michael @mimichael310
Cover Photo: Kimon Horne @_kimon
ISBN 978-0-9998291-7-2
Published by 310 Brown Street
www.310brownstreet.com
Earlthepoet.info@gmail.com
@theheartofearl

Huston-Tillotson University poet laureate, Earlyssa Cooper aka Earl the Poet, takes you on a journey through her family tree, up to the mountaintop where love dwells and back down to reality and new beginnings in her first published offering, "Never Put Down Your Pen."

TABLE OF CONTENTS

It's a Poet...Congratulations

I birthed my first baby in the fourth grade.

Teacher said it was beautiful,

and I'd make a good mother.

But she couldn't fathom how I was so broken,

but managed to produce

something so whole.

To fill the hole,

with my truth.

Which was in fact, just that,

I wrote to get away from my reality,

I wrote my way into a happier place.

So yes ma'am, now I do believe,

that pain does in fact birth poets.

Pain Births Poets

My SHERO

Mama took broken pieces in her bare hands,

but never had time to sit,

and watch her hands bleed…

At each of her fingertips birthed a new hustle,

a way to make ends meet.

Mama was my hero…

Long before I was introduced to Marvel

KNOCK

Am I in denial?

Am I running from the truth because it hurts too much to

look reality in the face?

Could it be that I'm not equipped for this pain?

This fight?

That life just drags me helplessly,

As things slide pass my window...

Like my grandma...

Oh, how I loved my grandma.

She used to teach me how to do things like,

Speak French,

Tie my shoe strings,

She even potty-trained me,

She taught me to SPEAK UP CLEARLY,

To make eye contact when I spoke so the other person

wouldn't think that I was playing.

She taught me to say what I mean,

And mean what I say,

To never let people push me around

To stand on my own two feet,

To hold my ground,

That if nobody around me believed in me,

SHE DID...

But what about the day she left me here?

The day I had to go bury her

and see her for the last time?

As a child that scarred me.

I knew she loved me,

Without a doubt,

I just...

I just...

Can't bear this pain,

So 'til this day, I tear up at the thought of her.

If I could just KNOCK on your casket,

Would you be able to hear me?

If I could just KNOCK on your casket,

Would you be able to hear me?

Have you ever missed somebody so much?

And couldn't do anything about it?

It's like you wanna be free,

Even if that means you have to die to see them again.

Without her, I'm missing a big part of me.

Know when I smile,

I'm covering my pain,

Because I've learned to accept the things I can't change.

Grab a pen and paper,

And jot this last thing down,

If you mourn too long from the backseat,

Your whole life might pass you by as the next tear is

falling down.

So use it as motivation,

And do it in remembrance of them.

But never stop,

Gain back control of your life,

So you can take the wheel

And drive.

More Like You, Jesus

I want to get to know the same God

that my grandma got down on her knees

and served for 68 years as she graced this earth

I want to know how it feels to have a faith so strong in

my God,

that I can be on my death bed suffering

after being a faithful servant for many years

and instead of being angry

I spent that time wrapped in God's word

knowing that his promises would never come back to me

voided

I want to get to know a God

that I can stand on top of a crate

and brag about to every person that I come across

matter-of-fact no,

I'd like for everyone I come across

to know that God lives in me,

just like he lived in my grandma.

Daddy's Little Girl

When I was in the 3rd grade we had donuts with dad.
When I was in the 6th grade, we had a father-daughter
dance... you missed both.
I'm not sure if it was hurt or hate that I had for you that
stirred me up on the inside
Or maybe I hated the fact that the person I loved the most
could hurt me with no remorse.

But this became a pattern, every year,
There was a new excuse to why you couldn't do
something.
I'd cry for hours, but the money you gave me helped
wipe the tears away.
Being called "spoiled" became a ritual for me and
everybody wanted a dad like just like *mine*.
Coming to drop off lunch, giving me the best birthdays,
making sure I had the latest sneakers,
or the hottest phone out
But man, if they only knew how I felt deep down inside,
Behind closed doors, daddy, I just wanted love

But maybe you played hide and go seek with your guilt

And maybe the money is how you always caught me

But maybe I accidently did it again, making excuses

again for you and the things you do.

Or let's talk about these "vacations" you'd go on

randomly, throughout the year.

See Grammy told me you'd be right back, but it was

never a turnaround trip.

I hated my mom the day she told me the truth that your

vacations consisted of you taking a trip in a squad car.

I thought she wanted me to hate you, so I hated her, but I

never really hated her, I hated the truth.

That no matter what you did I still loved you because I

was, and would always be, daddy's little girl.

Dear Drugs

Give me my daddy back!

I am bypassing him with this issue and coming straight to

you.

The eye of the hurricane.

The root of the problem!

You're not slick, you little skeezer you,

You know what you're doing when you're doing it,

Like a bad little kid sneaking into trouble when they

know better

Throwing the rock and then hiding your hand

I am here to beat you and kick you to the curb,

You are:

You are the reason why for many years,

Off and on my daddy's memories with me had to keep

me at night while he was away on "vacation" because he

got caught hanging with you and like a black mama

would say "that ain't your real friend."

You are the reason my grandma's tears hit the floor as she was on her knees lifting my dad's name in prayer, but before her prayer hit the ceiling he's already gone in the wind, giving in, getting high again.

I don't understand you, and I don't think I ever will.

You come in many equations, but the same common denominator is you ruin families.

On behalf of anyone else fighting this same battle with me against you.

I stand firm,

chest out,

eyes a little teary but my faith too strong.

I will fight you with every living breath in my body...

you will give my dad back to me.

You are a coward!

Look me back in my eyes and show some respect!

Don't come back and speak to me through my dad, when I've come straight to you.

Look me back in my eyes and listen carefully as I relay this message through you...the next time he's tempted to relapse, tell him "my brother, I can no longer serve you.

Your daughter said it was going to be either you or me and I really don't want you to have to choose."

Dear Drugs,
Give me my family back!
And I'm not gonna ask you again!

Reminiscing

2 Ears 1 second.

See Imma need your full attention,

I was told,

you're not grown 'til you're on your own,

and now I'm on my own,

and I'm not feeling too grown no more,

life sucka punched me

and knocked the wind out my mouth,

now I see exactly what those old folks use to warn me

about.

These bills rolling in like a wheelchair,

so every time a chair-bound person passes me by,

I just shake my head.

College is basically paying for school to get a job,

to get a job to pay for school.

It gets real out here.

Mama, I wanna come home,

but mama told me a long time ago that

once I left her house I was grown and on my own,

so I can't.

Now I'm sitting here tripping reminiscing on how in elementary school

we used to sit around and complain about the little stuff.

Took advantage of recess or those cat naps or

hold on wait a minute, those free snacks!

Because now...

We gotta buy everything!

In the real world, ain't no handouts B.

I'm fending for me,

you fending for you,

or what about how we rushed from elementary to middle school...

Talked to stupid and depreciated those teachers.

Then we jay walked into high school like we were the coolest, 'til our freshman tales were kicked off our high horses by upperclassmen.

But yet and still,

over the years we all found a place to belong.

We waited four years, on the one big day, of which we'd walk across the stage, signifying our first real milestone

in my cap and gown, I begin to stu- stu- stumble right
into the real world! And that door closed cold in my face
forever!

Santa,

      For Christmas, I want a time travel machine, so I
can go back into my past and actually enjoy those holiday
parties in elementary class, so I can relive my childhood
memories with my best friend, so I can laugh instead of
catch an attitude when I'm learning to color in the lines
because sooner than I think, those blue or black colored
pencils will turn into blue or black ink strictly for work
only. So, I can go back to recess, laughing, owing the
world no worries. Because sooner than I think, those
times will be gone.

Then I'm snatched back by my hair into reality
because you see my alarm clock just rang,
which means I have thirty minutes,
to get to a class across campus, for about two hours,
with a professor that barely knows my real name,
but you see…

that's a whole 'nother thang.

Moral of the poem, is to show y'all,

that over time, we fly through life,

not marinating in the moment,

but you see we'll keep on getting older,

and the world will keep on getting colder,

so now we're sitting here tripping man,

because we'll never be a kid again.

Dang.

Reality Check

As I transitioned from childhood to adulthood
it hit me like a tornado.
The inner kid stopped dreaming a long time ago.
And all the jumpers stood still.
If you've ever been around a child while you were going
through darkness,
you knew that there would be light again,
because the child's innocence reminded you of that.
The naive smile from ear to ear reminds you that every
day might not be a good day,
but it for sure has great moments,
a child's unfiltered comments remind us that over the
years, we've learned to filter our truths.
I challenge each of you,
whether it be at school,
or your job fair, or a new hobby,
or making that next big move you're hesitant to make....
DO IT! JUMP! JUMP WITHOUT THE FEAR OF
FAILING!!! JUMP WITH A HEART FULL OF HOPE!

JUMP LIKE YOU DON'T KNOW WHAT IT FEELS
LIKE TO FALL.

Become a dreamer again... dig out your inner fourth
grade kid filled with optimism and hope.

Because your life isn't over, until it ends.

Haiku:

Broken homes are where
wild flowers grow, because good
comes from broken things

Comparison Kills

When I was a child,

I'd run out of my house,

Stand on the tips of my toes

To see over my fence,

Just to stand in awe,

Because from a distance

Everyone else's grass seemed to be,

Greener, fuller, and more well-kept.

The craziest part is,

If the fence could've warned me back then,

when I was a child,

He'd whisper, "Adults make bad stuff look really good,

but the truth is we're all going through it."

The day after the fence spoke to me,

I stood in front of my mirror,

And repeated my newfound affirmations,

"The grass is greenest where I stand.

I must focus on my own garden to first make sure I am

well nourished,

With a good amount of sunlight.

For knowing this,

Will make all of my bad days,

A little better."

Self-worth isn't a transferrable energy.

Do You, Sis. They'll Judge You Regardless

Since the day of my birth,
I've been fighting to show white people I'm equal to
them.
Who are you?
Who are you to have the power and authority to make me
second guess my worth?
Who are you to make me feel ashamed of the melanin in
my skin?
Who are you to make me cringe inside based off of your
unwanted opinions?

I don't know who you are, but I do know who I am.
My resilience shines through in the darkest of rooms.
Turning the things that were meant to break me back
around in my favor.
I make struggle look good... struggles like getting picked
on for being a skin color in elementary school,
way before being light skinned or dark skinned became a
trend!

Having bigger features than my peers, like big lips and a big nose.

Being a curvy black girl automatically turns you into prey with most men.

Or how fighting the "angry black woman" stereotype has me walking on egg shells, when voicing my opinion turns into me being "loud and ghetto."

Or how people push you to your breaking point then wonder why you snap when all you are is human... too.

Being a carefree black girl means to be fearless, eccentric, courageous, and free spirited.

Embracing who you are on the inside.

No matter your size; skinny girls rock, and big girls do too.

So come out of your shell!

Shake the walls around you they tried to confine you in and let the world see your light.

Never be afraid to embrace the essence of your skin and personality...

which overflows in any room you are in.

There's no one way to black, we are unveiling the next Michelle Obamas, Maya Angelous, Whitney Houstons, and Viola Davis' right before our very eyes.

So, whether you wanna be "carefree" and still have your face beat you can do that!

Or if you wanna go natural with coconut oil you can do that too!

Being carefree doesn't mean to be careless,

but to care without regrets.

Caring less about what *they* say and finding your purpose in life.

So, whether you have kinky curls, box braids, a sew-in or rocking a bald fade...

I want you to know from the bottom of my heart to yours,

I LOVE YOU MY CAREFREE BLACK GIRLS WORLD WIDE

My Butterfly Babes

fighting the same battle as me, we will win.

Your life matters, you deserve to unapologetically be yourself, and to know you are not alone, and never will be.

Chin Up, Beautiful

Little girl,

dry your eyes, I can tell that you've been crying.

I can see your pain embedded on your face,

that you're way too stressed at such a young age,

pick your head up and

smile even when yesterday is too painful to forget,

and you're fearful for tomorrow.

Remember that God made you,

from him you are heaven sent.

Sometimes life has a way of knocking you down and

crippling your mind to think you will forever be nothing,

think again because you little girl, are unique.

Even when the negative seems to outweigh the positive.

Think outside the box.

Forget that, kick down that box, let me rephrase that kick

down those negative words that people have stacked

around you, secretly hoping you won't be a star.

There's a candle lit inside you that is begging to be
released so the world can know who you really are.
Stop letting people and the stupidity they speak fall into
your mind and change the way you think,
and how you view yourself.
Look in the mirror, dry your eyes,
I can tell that you've been crying...
Look into the same mirror and repeat after me,
"I am not what they say I am, instead I'm an art piece,
an untouched priceless antique.
God himself has handcrafted me.
My worth cannot be determined by anybody but me.
I am regaining control over my life from this day
forward.
I love myself and I am perfectly imperfect."
Little girl,
dry your eyes.
I can tell that you've been crying.
And I am only telling you this…
because, you are a little me.

Temple

When I shower, I can only wash for so long,

before I realize that I am embedded in my sin.

I've been in the bed, dancing with the devil

and I must admit,

I've enjoyed every minute of the twists, turns, dips, flips,

and turn arounds.

If you get my gist.

But it seems like whenever the sun lays down and it gets

dark, I am now drowning in thoughts that encase me.

My heart knows that this is wrong,

It's a temple they preach to me about at church.

And they were right…

My body is a temple

And I am the God it was built for,

I am the landlord

And I can let whoever I want live inside it,

Whenever.

You Listen

I remember the day I looked in the mirror

And although I didn't take a picture of this moment

It would forever be in my memory

My head held high

My chest poked out

Confident

That I was becoming the person I was meant to be...

You put your ear to the ground, and you listen!

To the flower growing from the concrete, the same

concrete that was walked on, and lied upon.

You put your ear to the ground, and you listen!

To every tear that I dropped on the ground,

collectively made a melody,

That people hum to not even knowing the full story.

You put your ear to the ground, and you listen!

To every splat of soil thrown by the shovel

As they prepare the tomb for that teenage suicide victim.

You put your ear to the ground, and you listen!

To those silent cries for help,

Death has escaped me countless times

When I never wanted it to leave in the first place.

You put your ear to the ground, and you listen!

To me climb over every obstacle,

And step on every problem that life throws my way.

I remember the day I looked in the mirror

And could honestly love what I saw looking back at me.

Can We Talk?

If we're being honest,

You scare me.

Because you're like a walking shadow of him.

Like I should go the other way.

Like I should know better…

Like your cologne smells all too familiar

so my stomach sinks to below sea level.

Like you too will sweeten me up,

Just to pull my sweet tooth

Like you're no better than my last dude,

Like I'm treading on the same thin ice,

Like I might hate school, but I know

you too have a master's degree in breaking women,

to build up your own alter ego.

Who are you fronting for?

You're running from your darkness

Just like me

I assume you're hopping from woman to woman to fill a
void.

But that woman fasho ain't me.

Take ya time, take ya time, one parked car convo and I'll
snatch ya mind.
I know imma rare breed,
But until I know my worth and tax these dudes,
They won't know how to treat nor handle me.

Parked Car Convos

She said, I wish you were a boy, so I could love you without feeling guilty, because in the back of my head I know that this is wrong.

She said, you show me the love, support and compassion that I'm trying to teach him how to show me.

How do you do it so effortlessly, she said I'm falling for you like Leela James, can you promise to catch me?

I took her for a swim at 4AM,

Promising not to leave her in the deep end,

How my conversation in parked car sessions,

Allowed her to search deep and,

Even if she let go, I would still be there.

That she could trust me.

She said I wish you were a boy, so I could love you limitlessly, but my love for you has boundaries. Friends are what we are, and probably all we're meant to be.

And that night I went to sleep wishing I were a boy, so I could love her the way she yearned to be loved...

unconditionally.

Location: Somewhere

Can you come over tonight and just hold me? Can you act like every word you spoke held weight under it and it wasn't just floating? I've heard I love you before, but not many have shown it. I asked you when you walked in my world to be gentle with my heart for the last time it was stirred up it was left unsettled. I'm starting to hate love because love has yet to love me back... I've become bitter, to the subject, to the feeling, to the guy that rekindles that old flame with no intentions on enjoying my company as it burns. Like old canned goods, my love was tossed to the back and recycled. I didn't meet the qualifications yet again. I must've missed a part in the "how to love" book for dummies. Another night filled with teary eyes and regrets. I just wait up on the sunrise, for the new day leaves room to hide the night's madness. I just want to escape. But where do you go when everyone's running? From their own darkness, and truth.

Read 3:08am

Calm Before the Storm

I love,

much like the rain.

Sometimes really lightly,

but when I believe you need it,

my love will pour down on you.

Without warning,

or permission.

Some hate the rain,

but it's on a mission,

to stop you from getting

too overwhelmed

from the heat,

fake love will warm you up,

and hold you close,

just to make you feel,

disgusting, and sweaty.

And even the people that don't like rain,

still enjoy hearing it.

So,

I ask you,

whether you enjoy dancing in the rain,

or listening to it hit your window pane.

Will you at least be open?

I Hope It's Just A Nightmare

The second time around,

I didn't fight back,

This part of the movie was all too familiar to me,

So, I didn't push him away,

I didn't scream no,

I whispered it,

I laid there,

I switched my mindset to "get it over with" mode

Before he could switch to "I was going to do it anyway"

This time I knew the dirty feeling,

The helpless thoughts,

Would be coming shortly afterwards

But I knew how to ignore them this go round.

If your first attacker got away with it,

Wouldn't the second one too?

Because we all know three is a lucky number

And good fortune has always missed me.

If I had to describe it the best way I could

I'd say it's like the second bite of food,

From the least most enjoyable item on your plate,

You're forced to do it.

I knew my part,

I knew how to play it,

I mean, I have sex all the time,

So, the one time I didn't want it… shouldn't matter right?

They'll say I'm always loud so why was I so quiet about this?

They'll ask me what *I* was wearing.

And why was *I* alone? I was in my own home...

And if we're being honest,

Unless you've experienced the humility,

You won't understand the words that I speak.

He's still out there free,

Because I never mustered up the courage to speak,

So yeah, screw the men that go around stealing vagina

When there's so many women who would give it up for free. You're the weakest form of man to me.

Flowers

He told me "you are hard to love"

And it was right in that moment,

I realized,

He'd fell in love with my flowers

Before he ever acknowledged my roots.

To love a rose

Is to understand how it grew the way it grew.

Childhood trauma.

Word Vomit

I didn't say I loved you first, when I knew I did...on purpose. Because I've had love bombard into my home with no prior warning it was coming, but I allowed it to stay. Toxicity stopped it from growing, but I didn't want to be robbed of my time, so I compromised.

Good Intentions

They saw a cute face,

wrapped in a smooth charisma,

confidence that only existed through other people's

compliments.

They labeled you "that nigga,"

so "that nigga" is who you proclaimed.

Nobody else knew this Nupe was broken before he came

to me?

Mama left a hole in your heart your first semester of

college,

so without knowing it,

you transferred that same hole into every woman you

would later meet.

They whispered and warned me to run,

I'm 100% sure God whispered louder and said you

needed me.

To plant my 2 feet down, and stick it out with you,

not to be naive enough to believe I wouldn't be

mistreated in the process

but to take my time to figure out the reason for your
destructiveness.

I was never afraid of you breaking me, because I met you
as a whole on my own.

I was ready for this task.

Through time, patience and prayer, God promises us
through his word, he's able to make old things new again.

When I first laid my eyes on you,

I could see you were a lost soul.

The bags under your eyes gave it away clear as day

you carry loads far heavier than just your own.

I knew you weren't ready,

so I never intended to fall for you.

I knew I would have to first know you in and out,

before I could help.

But I knew I could only reach the sober you, so we would
first start with your drinking.

What were you looking for at the bottom of your cup?

Did you get messed up to cover up the internal junk?

Or the emotional trauma?

Or being big brother and daddy all tied up in one?

Hey! Look at me, stop crying!

We'll get through this,

one day at a time.

In June, I snatched the demon you'd battled for the last 7

years out of you,

he knows he's not welcome back in our home!

You've overcome one of your struggles and I couldn't be

any prouder.

I didn't plan to fall for you 218 days ago,

But I don't regret that I did.

Because real love has found me.

But remember this, if you forget everything else I've

said...

In you, Nupe, are poems that aren't meant to be read by

everyone.

You are a GOD fearing, family loving man.

You're not that nigga.

That label takes away value from the real you.

I love you, and I wanna keep bringing out and revealing

to you, the best parts of you...

and every day I roll over and say good morning,

remember THIS is my promise to you.

Man Hunt!

Today the suspect we're looking for identifies as:

A *black woman*,

Young,

Standing at about *5'9*,

Weighing roughly *140 pounds,*

She's **armed and dangerous**!

I repeat she is **armed and dangerous!**

She's killed well over 50 men.

She's heartless,

She won't stop until we find her!

The trick is,

She's a pro at reversing intentions.

Right when you think you have her locked down,

She'll slip right from beneath your fingertips.

Like she's not fond of handcuffs,

It's as if she's numb to feeling,

Like she never stays long enough,

to feel at all.

I've noticed her pattern in her victims…

She doesn't target dark skinned men,

Only light skinned ones,

The reason is unbeknownst to us at the moment.

All of the victims range from 6'0 to 6'10,

Clearly, she is not a fan of midget men.

They all range between early and mid-20s,

Tatted from head to heels,

They hold the physique of either a current or former athlete,

Who has obtained the statuses and education that qualifies them to be,

"too smart" to be dead, so why them?

When we dusted the bodies for fingerprints

They were nowhere to be found except,

On the chest of the victims

It almost seems like she enjoys killing egotistical men

But what was her motive?

When we arrived at the crime scene

The victims were spread out wide,

With sunflowers in the palms of both hands,

Laid out like the crucifixion,

This was his sacrifice to man.

Unopened condoms,

That would never be used again.

The ribs seemed to be the only thing on the body left

bruised and battered.

When we checked her background

It was squeaky clean with no traces of being violent in

her past

We did find out she'd been abused in her adolescence

She was used to being silenced and feeling unwanted,

And told from a man,

That she would never be good enough.

Perhaps this was retaliation.

Perhaps this was the method to her madness.

We just received a call from our tip line***

She's been spotted in front of a church

Yelling at the top of her lungs:

"GOD IF THIS IS MY BODY, AND IT'S A TEMPLE,

HOW AM I NOT THE GOD THAT IT WAS BUILT

FOR? I'M TIRED YANNO! I'M SORRY TOO! I
CONFESS THAT I KILLED THOSE MEN BECAUSE I
WASN'T CLOSE ENOUGH TO YOU! TO TEACH
THEM A LESSON THAT ONLY YOU CAN… THAT
YOU DON'T MEET A WOMAN, ACT LIKE YOU
LOVE HER, JUST TO HAVE SEX WITH HER! I'M
SORRY! I HOPE THAT YOU CAN STILL HEAR A
SINNER'S PRAYER!!!!"

She pleaded guilty in court,

Said that the fingerprints she left on her victims

were actually soul ties,

But she didn't know it then,

Now they were growing to be too much for her,

She believed she would be more content in her solitude.

She needed a break,

Before she broke.

Perhaps this was her last resort,

To practice,

Celibacy.

Dear Anonymous

You were more secure on your own but,

but when nighttime came,

darkness whispered to you,

And reminded you how lonely you were

So eventually you gave in

And allowed yourself to settle for a physical body,

but really the soul was absent

And true feelings were never there

Y'all created soul ties with raw sex

And temporary talks about the future

So, your mind had something to cling to,

but was it love, or lust from the jump?

The first time he put his hands on you

You tricked your mind

With the help of him

Into believing it would never happen again...

And it doesn't for a while

The apology actually seems genuine

And it's followed by changed behavior

But you can't seem to silence

The inner warrior beating on the inside of your belly

Also referred to as:

Your gut feeling,

your intuition

your spirit of discernment

Or simply my mama didn't raise boo-boo the fool!

All screaming you should leave when the first red flag

came rolling in,

With sirens connected to it.

But I have a question

How do you leave when your mind has the common

sense to run

but your heart,

Your heart controls your feet?

You literally are stuck in "love" right?

You walked with too much confidence

So, it made insecure people uneasy every time you were

in the same room as them

So, they had two options:

Never share the same room as you or

Break you down until you are silent.

Secretly transferring over all their insecurities.

You avoided every mirror for a month straight

Trying to silence the voices repeating those negative

affirmations

That have been implanted in your head

Waiting to bloom into newly found self-doubt.

You've been yelling through a bullhorn

in a crowd full of people

That you would go to war for this person

When in actuality this person was at war with themselves

And you

And you were at war with everyone else defending them.

Take off your armor

Step back

Get fresh air into your lungs

And walk away

Before you are killed in the crossfire.

Because love never hurts like this.

And you were never anonymous

You were simply a woman.

If darkness was meant to last forever, you would never see the end of the tunnel.

Please Keep Fighting; We Need You Here

Suicide is tugging on the back of her shirt
like the cold December's breeze, she…
doesn't wanna breathe.
Some think it's for attention,
but after the spotlight fades away,
and the show ends,
she's crying backstage,
because this was not a part of the play.
She did not audition for this role,
it just happened!

Daytime has become the platform for her night's
madness,
plotting in the sunlight, but when the dawn breaks,
she's attacking herself
clothes can't hide the wounds she's afflicted on herself
she covers it up in designer,
like she's in a fashion show for us,
but she's running from her problems like she's in the
Olympics.

I wish our generation wasn't so ignorant,

maybe then she wouldn't feel so empty,

secretly soul searching

and seeking to find the next sista's secret,

because this has really become a competition,

if she isn't thicker or skinnier than this sista, she's

considered ugly.

She looks in the mirror and pinpoints her flaws,

wanting to disappear in her mirror's reflection,

she begins to wish she were a snake to shed the extra

skin.

You can't compare their load to yours,

we are all battling.

Although sometimes family situations seem unbearable

you have to keep pushing,

if darkness were meant to last forever, you would never

see the end of the tunnel

If you need someone to talk to,

I promise God got you,

if you feel like he's been quiet in the midst of your storm,

I can assure you he's already got it handled.

I wish you could take a peek at you from another person's point of view.

Suicide not only affects you, but everybody directly connected to you.

Remember: Love is one of the few things that multiplies the more you give it away.

#MAKING POETS IMMORTAL

310 BROWN STREET
.com

PUBLISHING